Washington

A PORTRAIT OF THE EVERGREEN STATE

foreword by
PAUL DORPAT

Washington

A PORTRAIT OF THE EVERGREEN STATE

foreword by
PAUL DORPAT

PIPELINE BOOKS

Published by Pipeline Books, 8030 South 228th Street, Kent, Washington 98032-2900, in cooperation with SkyHouse Publishers, an imprint of Falcon Press Publishing Company, Helena, Montana.

Design, typesetting, and other prepress work by SkyHouse Publishers, Helena, Montana.

Printed and bound in Korea.

Library of Congress Catalog Number 94-68053

ISBN 1-885369-00-X (paper)
ISBN 1-885369-02-6 (cloth)

Distributed to the trade by Pacific Pipeline. To order, write to 8030 South 228th Street, Kent, Washington 98032-2900; call toll free 1-800-677-2222; or fax toll-free 1-800-873-0849.

Text set in Adobe Minion.

FRONT COVER: A ferry crosses Puget Sound at sunset, the Olympic Mountains in the distance. GARY L. BENSON/ALLSTOCK.

Photographed from Harbor Drive, Seattle's skyline catches the day's last light. TERRY DONNELLY.

"*I was born in the State of Washington and I have lived there for almost forty years, off and on. I have regarded it from the perspective of Manhattan and Canada, the Aleutians and Mexico, Los Angeles and New Orleans. I still am not sure just what it is, in addition to being a great piece of land of almost unlimited possibilities. I do not know whether it is a way of life or a state of mind, and I think it is a little of both.*"

NARD JONES
Evergreen Land
A Portrait of the State of Washington, 1947

Lupine and Indian paintbrush beneath the Tatoosh Range, Mount Rainier National Park.   CHARLES GURCHE.

Foreword

*I*n my second grade classroom, an oval-framed print of George Washington hung to the left of the Washington state map. I struggled with fitting—twisting really—that face into the outline of the state. After considerable effort, aided mightily by the tools of reverie, I managed it. George Washington and Washington state fit together, at least, much better than did Abraham Lincoln and the state's outline. The Great Emancipator's portrait hung to the right of the map. And now, while preparing to write this introduction to *Washington: A Portrait of the Evergreen State*, I wonder if the other kids came to the same conclusion. This triptych of two presidents and a map was once, I imagine, a commonplace in the primary schools of Washington state. Is there deep in those of us who learned our ABCs here an intuition that what Washington state looks like is a heroic Virginian with thin lips, a receding hairline interrupted by a white wig, and an unfinished collar?

I can imagine that the editors and publisher of this book must also have struggled to fit this state with a portrait. Ask Washingtonians what it is about the place that is worth featuring and they will usually answer the obvious—its variety. Of course, this claim is commonplace for practically any place, the other Washington included. But here we're talking about our variety.

This Washington hasn't had nearly as many heroes as the other Washington. But if we are counting our intrepid, I'd include the photographers who contributed to this book. Trekking after the state's picturesque, grand, wild, enchanting features, they reveal the imagination of our landscape. It is a decidedly humble heroism, for here it is Washington that distinguishes its Washingtonians. It is the place that exalts us all. Some of the most sophisticated yet steady Washingtonians hardly ever leave their state. They are too busy exploring it.

Photographs, of course, cannot give us the names of things—except on signs. The state's place names are its first portraiture. In the beginning only spoken, the native names reveal our ancient faces. Spokane means "children of the sun"; Cathlamet means "stone" for the Columbia's rocky Cathlamet Channel; Chelan, "deep water"; Humptulips, for the river which is "hard to pole"; and so on and on. Next the explorers, Spanish and English, came and named, and they were followed by the merchants, American, English, and with the English the French. Nez Perce, Palouse, Nisqually, are all the additions of French Canadians, most of them in the employ of the Hudson Bay Company. Finally, the American settlers arrived and from them a proliferation of names fills the state's official catalogue with most of its entries, at last count about 31,519. A rule of thumb says that these authorized names represent about one-third of the names actually in common use here. And this still is not the whole of it—street names are not included.

Evergreen State, our nickname, is not that new. Charles Conover, a Seattle reporter and real estate developer, coined it while doing publicity for Washington when it gained statehood in 1889. Of course, Washington is not merely green, and sometime ago the state legislature added gold to green for the state colors. Actually, it's somehow dotty to think of Washington having official colors. We have also a Red Pass, a Yellow Lake, Blue Mountains, a Silver Forest—a "ghost forest" of fire-bleached trunks in Mount Rainier National Park—and at least nine Silver Creeks and nine Silver Lakes. Like the state's poets, landscape artists, and the photographers whose work appears here, the solons should have kept adding colors, for there are enough hues within these borders to make the color chips that overflow the sample cases at your paint store seem merely official.

There are no residential requirements to run for office in Washington state, but you must register to vote thirty days before state elections. But how long does it take to become a Washingtonian? I would say on the average about a week—some sooner, some later. When you understand the imagination of this place, you become distinguished by it, and that's when you become a Washingtonian. Ultimately, because of Washington's spectacular variety, it is strange even to those who are most familiar with it, the sons and daughters of its pioneers. Precocious tourists can become Washingtonians. Even readers can cross the threshold. You must simply submit, and stay on the trail.

Washington state does have its snobs, but they generally hurl their snubs at one another. This volleying is most congested over the Cascades Mountains, across which the partisans of the state's wet and dry sides may throw mud balls and rocks, respectively. It can get nasty. I, for one, believe that there should be a test for some Washingtonians. State residents inclined towards snide or peevish snobbery should be required to sing the state's anthem, "Washington My Home." Made to render lyrics like "There's peace you feel and understand, in this our own beloved land" and "Small towns and cities, rest here in the sun. Filled with our laughter, they will be done," they will either lighten up or be tapped to sing again. But by far, most Washingtonians are not snobs about their state. We're disposed to variety, not exclusivity.

Naturally, Washington has its experts. Imagine a round table of them, the state's most distinguished disciples, living and revived, gathered together at Justice William O. Douglas's home on Goose Prairie. Let them struggle to arrive at some wise consensus about which features are essential for any depiction of the state. We may imagine our panel moderated by Edward R. Murrow. Cartoonist Gary Larson could make sketches of all attending—including their pets—and Bing Crosby could provide the entertainment, probably to grunge accompaniment. Bruce Lee could stand guard—although we wouldn't need one at Goose Prairie—and Bill Gates could pay for it. (If requested, there could be a D. B. Cooper fly-by.) I would propose substantial honorariums for such attendees as Murray Morgan,

who has written histories of just about every part of Washington; Fred Beckey, who by now has probably climbed all its mountains; Ruth Kirk, who has traveled all its back roads and written intelligently about what she found there; Archie Satterfield, who has done much the same; and Jim Faber, partly because I'd like to see him again. Faber's *Irreverent Guide to Washington* is as good-humored as he was himself. To be fair, there are many others who should attend, but I'll leave it at that—except for Miss Dorothy Larson, my first grade teacher in Grand Forks, North Dakota.

It was Miss Larson who introduced me to Washington moments before Dad got his call to move us there. As I remember it, my teacher was absolutely in the thrall of Mount Rainier and kept a picture of it in the World Book opened on her desk. However, the effect of Miss Larson's enthusiasm was to stir in me a great feeling of deprivation. I suspect that the want of mountains may be the universal desire of midwestern kids, before they are trained to substitute anything beyond the barn—like a haystack. So when Dad, the Reverend Theodore Ertman Dorpat, got his call to leave the Lutherans of Grand Forks for those in Spokane and we headed west in our new 1946 Plymouth sedan, I kept my eyes open for Mount Rainier. It first broke the horizon a few miles west of Billings. But when Mother, our navigator, unfolded her map and demonstrated that the Beartooth Mountains of Montana were still 450 miles east of Washington, the heart of this future Washingtonian was momentarily broken on the broken lands of the Upper Missouri Basin.

At 1818 West Ninth on Spokane's South Hill, the church parsonage was two and a half blocks from a dead-end bluff high above Hangman Creek. There, where the sunsets are often retouched by the dust blown east from the farms and scablands of the Columbia Basin, I quickly learned that Washington is much more than its highest point. And now, although I've lived in Seattle for nearly thirty years and am even now looking at Mount Rainier from my desk, whenever I travel beyond state borders and am asked where I'm from, I surrender to an uncanny reflex to answer Spokane. And with every visit of friends and family in my old home town, I return to the neighborhood on Ninth and its dead end and view west into the Big Bend.

With all the experience, intelligence, imagination, and vital connections our round table would bring to their consensus, they would, no doubt, humbly conclude, first, that Washington is a state anyone—including our experts—can get lost in and, second, that they should. We might open this book before the panel. Surely some of them would be unfamiliar with some of its scenes. However, they would no doubt agree that all its pages intimate Washington.

Below, I will benignly boom about a few of this state's features. As a historian I will sometimes note how they have been used and, on occasion, abused. First, in a brief portrait of Washington's Big Picture, this is the list of its distinctions, of its parts that are not repeated in any combination anywhere else in the world: Puget Sound, the "Mediterranean of the Pacific"; the Columbia River, the "River of the West"; the Palouse farmlands, the "Breadbasket of the West"; the Cascades, the "Alps of America," distinguished by the most painted and photographed mountain in America; the Columbia Basin scablands, a result of the "world's greatest flood"; the Olympic Peninsula, with the world's most complete temperate rain forest; and the Washington coastline, with its protected harbors.

Captain James Cook missed our harbors. His map shows our coast as a squiggle—part of a line which runs continuously from San Francisco Bay to Friendly Cove on Vancouver Island. Sailing north in 1778 from Cape Foulweather on today's Oregon coast, Cook missed the Columbia River, Willapa Harbor, Grays Harbor, and the Strait of Juan de Fuca. He nearly entered the strait when, for a moment through the fog, he thought he detected an opening in the coastline. The cape which interrupted these blandishments Cook named Flattery. So Cook missed the strait, and his ship *Resolution* was soon driven off shore by a squall. The future Washington remained a terra incognito to the English explorer.

On board the *Resolution* was a teenaged seaman named George Vancouver. Years later when Vancouver prepared to embark on his own voyage of discovery, the British Admiralty provided no artist for his exploration, apparently believing that Cook had drawn everything in the world that needed to be copied. But with at least five of his regular crew claiming some drafting talent, Vancouver was permitted to carry drawing paper and ink. After the Indian petroglyphs, the results are the oldest extant portraits of Washington state. There may have been earlier sketches made of its shores by the few Spanish explorers and English merchants that sailed along the north coast in the years between Cook's voyage and Vancouver's return. They have not, however, survived.

Among the subjects sketched by Vancouver's amateurs was what his log notes as the "round snowy mountain" that he named "after my friend Rear Admiral Rainier." The log date was May 8, 1792. Although imperfect like Vancouver's charts of Puget Sound, the expedition's drawing of "The Mountain" is very readable, if unrealistic. It is too pointed, and on its eastern flank, Little Tahoma—which at 11,117 feet is the third highest peak in the state—is reduced to a foothill of the big Mount Tahoma or Tacoma.

Once upon a time on the streets of Tacoma, it was heresy to use any but the Indian name for the "round snowy mountain," which is roughly what "Tacoma" means. Authentic, euphonious, and patriotic was Tacoma. Larcenous, dissonant, and alien was Rainier —the Brit who never saw the mountain and who even fought against American patriots during the Revolutionary War. In a fit of English patriotism the unwed admiral left most of his estate to help pay his country's debts. The century-long controversy over the name of the mountain between the advocates of Tacoma and Rainier is one of the great serio-comedies of state history, and so part of its historical portrait.

From every angle Mount Rainier adds grandeur to scenes which might otherwise be merely picturesque. Mount Rainier is the cardinal feature of the state. It's not merely the mountain's height that stands out, but how the mountain reaches that prominence as it rises from sea level, hoary and majestically alone. Scenes which might include it must have it. Postcard artists, especially, regularly collage or clarify the mountain in photographs where clouds or smog erase it. In colored postcards, sunsets on the mountain may seem screened through a filter of jelly beans.

A climber's camp in Boston Basin, Boston Peak, North Cascades National Park. PAT O'HARA.

Understandably, Mount Rainier is easily the most recorded subject in the Pacific Northwest. This taste reaches from the sublime art of early-century painter-photographers Albert Henry Barnes of Tacoma and Norman Edson of Vashon Island to the paint-by-number Rainier copyrighted by the wife of an unemployed lumberjack and sold with other souvenir knick-knacks in the shadow of the mountain. Arthur Churchill Warner was the first photographer to reach the 14,411-foot-summit. Invited to record naturalist John Muir's first ascent in 1888, Warner managed to lug his clumsy view camera up the mountain and with the others reach Columbia Crest near noon on August 14, 1888. Warner used his coat for a focusing cloth and nearly froze his arms in the process.

Seattle School Superintendent E. S. Ingraham was part of Muir's party; in fact, he impatiently led it. Ingraham was one of the mountain's first experts. He made several ascents, wrote the first guide book, and named many of Rainier's features including Gibraltar Rock, Columbia Crest, Elysian Fields, and Camp Muir. There are plenty of difficult ways to climb Rainier, but the easiest takes about eight hours from Camp Muir. At a little over the 10,000-foot level and only four miles above Paradise, Camp Muir is the staging ground for the hundreds of climbers who attempt the summit each summer, trampling the route into a trail.

Reaching the summit can, on occasion, be too fantastic—especially for those who spend the night huddled for warmth inside the crater's sulfuric ice caves. In his 1894 guide book, the ordinarily sober Ingraham tells how, while deep in the crater, he fell "within the influence of a mysterious glow" emitting from a grotesque crawling figure with pointed eyeballs. By means of a light or electric charge that arced between them, Ingraham "communicated" with the "Old Man of the Crater" who told of an ancient race of humanoids that lived within the mountain. Again, Ingraham was quick with a name, calling them "Sub-Rainians."

Years later, Ingraham's Old Man of the Crater was

followed by flying saucers. The international enthusiasm for UFOs began in 1947 above the southern slopes of Mount Rainier when a pilot from Boise, Idaho, reported nine disk-like lights hurtling through the air. Three decades later, after a proliferation of sightings and close encounters, a Tacoma group calling itself the New Age Foundation opened a fourteen-acre Interplanetary Neutral Zone just outside the park entrance and outfitted it with a landing strip for space ships. These too are Washingtonians.

For the Indians on Puget Sound, George Vancouver's *Discovery* was probably not an altogether unidentified object. Word of the several voyages along the Northwest Coast that followed Cook's in 1778 must have reached them before Captain Vancouver actually sailed into the sound. To the English explorer, Puget Sound was beautiful and hospitable. The description from his log is the first, best known, and most often reprinted "pen picture" of Puget Sound. His eulogy is so charmed it reads almost like wedding oratory.

To describe the beauties of this region, will, on some future occasion, be a very grateful task to the pen of a skillful panegyrist. The serenity of the climate, the innumerable pleasing landscapes, and the abundant fertility that unassisted nature puts forth, require only to be enriched by the industry of man with villages, mansions, cottages and other buildings, to render it the most lovely country that can be imagined; while the labour of the inhabitants would be amply rewarded, in the bounties which nature seems ready to bestow on cultivation.

Had the enchanted captain lingered to plant a garden, he would have discovered that the gravel and clay left by the retreating glaciers grow better Douglas-fir and red cedar than carrots and green beans. The exceptions on the east shore of Puget Sound are the wide valleys where the silt of the Cascades has been deposited over flood plains as fertile as Vancouver's vision. Perhaps the Skagit Valley best fulfills his reverie. There, as the loggers cut eastward into the foothills, they exposed bottomlands with topsoil deeper than a tall Swede's shoulders. The farmers followed and cultivated a cul-

ture of peas, beans, corn, and tulips. Today, tourists, many on bikes, pursue the tulips.

While the recent bi-centennial of Vancouver's exploration didn't arouse the fuss of the state's 1989 centennial, it did permit us to imagine what Peter Puget, Joseph Whidbey, Joseph Baker, and the rest of Vancouver's crew would think of us now. Our most distinguished landmark, the state capitol, would seem familiar to them because they knew so well one of the great European buildings it was modeled after: St. Paul's Cathedral in London. However, before you can sight from off Dofflemyer Point the capitol campus, you must sail a long way south from Admiralty Inlet. And what would Vancouver and his crew think of the Kingdome?

On the whole we might suspect that George Vancouver would find this the "lovely country" he imagined. Surely, the evidences of this Washington portrait would confirm his intimation. While Washington state, as we Euro-Americans have cultivated it, is surely no Eden, it is, at least, in many parts Edenic. Now we have time to enjoy the noble, sublime, picturesque, grand, wild, enchanting, curious, and humorous qualities of our state. However, we should remember that both our leisure and mobility were built upon the backs of the pioneers. And so we should recall them.

Until awakened by the depressing events of the Indian wars in the mid 1850s, the pioneers who first settled north of the Columbia in the late 1840s had only the haziest notion of what they were in for. It required tough work to cut holes in the rain forests and draw water from the dry lands. It was later, after the Northern Pacific Railroad began surveying the mountain passes in 1869, that Washingtonians became generally reflective, sometimes obsessed, and more and more crafty about their territory's assets.

Washington's first boomers, the real estate and railroad agents and town builders, emphasized the salubrious ease of this place, the gentle rains, its freedom from malaria, the bountiful game, and its great river, the "River of the West"—the mighty Columbia. Puget Sound developed its own cliche: the "Mediterranean of the Pacific" where, when the tides retreated, the table was set. The boomers' optimism nourished the new immigrants' own hopes to make a new life in a new Eden, leaving the Old Adam behind in St. Louis and New York. But muckraking editors were quick to point out that a variety of Old Adams came west as well.

Perhaps the only immigrant to find an Eden, of sorts, in Washington was the devout Willie Keil. A roadside marker near Willie's grave in Pacific County tells his story. The teenager and his parents were members of the Bethel Colony: Christian communalists who shared all in common. Four days before the colony's train of sixty-one persons left Bethel, Missouri, for the Oregon Trail, Willie died of malaria. Instead of driving the lead wagon, Willie rode in a zinc-lined casket mounted in a wagon carefully fixed to resemble a hearse. Thus, immersed in alcohol, Willie Keil led the immigrants west, and on November 26, 1855, he was buried on a hill above the Willapa River.

The Bethels arrived in Washington two years after President Franklin Pierce awarded a new territory to those who had already settled north of the Columbia River. Earlier, the English fur traders and merchants at Fort Vancouver on the Columbia and Fort Nisqually on Puget Sound had peacefully, albeit reluctantly, agreed to move beyond the 49th parallel, where the northern border of the future state was set in 1846. Columbia, the name suggested by its applicants, was amended away by a Representative Richard H. Stanton of Kentucky who thought that christening the territory after its great river would create bureaucratic mayhem in the District of Columbia. So, in a clear instance of the right brain not knowing what the left brain is doing, the other Washington substituted Washington for Columbia. Stephen A. Douglas's contention that Washington be lengthened to Washingtonia got little support. Douglas's alternative would have made us feel less clumsy about referring to ourselves as Washingtonians, but the senator from Illinois was, alas, already losing his debates.

Lieutenant Charles Wilkes, the American Vancouver, charted Puget Sound in 1841. Along with the pressure of American homesteaders moving north of the Columbia River, Wilkes's hydrography was calculated to muscle the English north of the 49th parallel. The often imperial lieutenant combined his patriotic assignment with a naming binge. Mount Constitution on Orcas Island is the highest point in the San Juans. Wilkes named it for the U.S.S. Constitution, or "Old Ironsides," the 204-foot frigate that won many battles against the British during the War of 1812. (Wilkes also named Bainbridge Island after the ship's captain, William Bainbridge.) In 1935 employees of the Civilian Conservation Corps—the "CCC Boys"—built the striking 52-foot-high granite tower on the summit. It is one of the finest public-works creations of the Great Depression, and the full-circle view from its observatory—from Vancouver Island to Mount Rainier and from the Canadian Cascades to the Olympics—is beyond ratings. The 2,409-foot summit can be reached by car. Count the steps to the top of the tower.

From the Pacific Ocean, the Olympic Mountains are the profile of Washington's portrait. The fastest way to climb them is up Hurricane Ridge, ten miles south of Port Angeles. There one looks across the Elwha River valley to the impressive wall of the Bailey Range named for William E. Bailey, owner of *The Seattle Press* and sponsor of the 1890 press expedition into the steep, dense, and wet heart of the peninsula. At this writing, 104 years and several hundred miles of trails later, hiking is still the best way to visit the Olympics. But stay on the trail.

Urban hiking is a favorite pastime of Seattleites, and it's aerobic. The city has more than five hundred public stairways. Seattle is a city of undulating ridges, spines carved by the same ice that shaped British Columbia's Gulf Islands and Washington's San Juans. So it's a city of view lots, and real estate prices reflect this. The most common of the many ways to view the city skyline are probably also the best: prospects from West Seattle, site of the original settlement; Queen Anne Hill, looking across Seattle Center, the site of the 1962 Century 21 World's Fair; and Beacon Hill. From Beacon Hill, especially on a late summer evening, Seattle's modern cityscape can put on a show. The glow of a northern sunset and the lights of the freeway reflect against the glass, steel, and polymer curtains of the central business district. It is not an Emerald City then. The many colors scattered from the skyline resemble a diadem and suggest the name "Queen City" used here for a century until emerald was rudely substituted by contest.

The Columbia SeaFirst Center is the highest building north of Los Angeles—actually it has more floors but fewer feet than L.A.'s First Interstate Bank Building—and the twentieth highest building in the world. The public observation level is not on the structure's seventy-sixth or top floor. That is reserved for a club whose membership, I'm told, includes Seattle's most ascendant cliff dwellers. Rather, the public elevator stops a few floors below, which—it seems to me—is still too high. From there the Smith Tower with its pyramidal top resembles a paper weight. When it was completed in 1914, the Smith Tower was a beacon to sailors and at forty-two stories the highest building west of . . . New York, Chicago, or the Mississippi, depending upon which promotion you read. The Smith Tower's terracotta elegance was well promoted nationwide and was the first best evidence that Washingtonians did not all live and work in hollowed-out cedar stumps. For Seattle panoramas, it is my favorite observation platform. You look up to the city's new towers and down to its many historic neighborhoods, including the International District, Pioneer Square, the central waterfront, and the Pike Place Market. To actually take hold of Seattle, it's important to return to ground and visit those places.

Construction of the Smith Tower began only 71 years after Elliott Bay was first settled by Euro-Americans, less than 150 years ago. Although the University of Washington Library's Special Collections Division gets the occasional request for a photograph of the 1851 landing of the Denny Party at Alki Point, there was no photographer waiting in the rain on shore for the Dennys and Borens and the rest of their party. But there could have been. The midwesterners came by way of the Oregon Trail and Portland, and revealing photographs of the Rose City's main street survive from that time.

We will probably never know who snapped the first photograph of any Washington subject, but it was most likely along the Columbia River, perhaps a portrait of an officer at Fort Vancouver.

Seattle's first photographer was a young school teacher, E. A. Clark. With his back to Henry Yesler's steam sawmill, Clark photographed Sara Yesler on the front porch of the couple's home in the Pioneer Square area. It was 1859, seven years after most of the community's original settlers had moved from Alki Point to the east shore of Elliott Bay.

Popular pioneer subjects included rhododendrons, heaps of salmon, piles of ducks, huge stumps, oversize vegetables, watermelon feasts, and of course, houses, portraits, main streets, and Indians—especially Indians. It is said that they were shot twice—first by the cavalry and then by photographers. The best known of the snap-shooters was the Seattle photographer, Edward Curtis. While encyclopedic, his work is controversial because of the often theatrical settings he gave his subjects and the poses he directed them to take. A matter of taste, the value of Curtis's photography will be argued eternally. But it is emphatically a vital part of Washington's historical portrait.

Perhaps Edward Curtis is to Indians as the Washington mountain communities of Leavenworth and Winthrop are to Bavaria and the Old West respectively. Since the opening of the North Cascades Highway, Winthrop has improved its western facades for visitors to "America's Alps" and the more than three hundred glaciers of North Cascades National Park. Leavenworth, on the Stevens Pass Highway, is like a theme park with its Tyrolean facades and Oom-Pah-Pah celebrations, which are a pleasure for those who enjoy the themes. Leavenworth is also the back door to the Alpine Lakes Wilderness Area, including the emerald tarns and mist-swept crags of the remote Enchantments which, according to many of Washington's experienced mountaineers, are what they claim: the most enchanting landscape in the state.

The halloos of promotion were commonplace in the advertisements of Washington's pioneer towns. My favorite for bull and bluster is Cascade City. About seven miles southwest of Lind beside the mainline of the Northern Pacific, Cascade City was platted in 1892. A map detailing its blocks and lots was printed alongside an artist's birdseye view of an idyllic community of parks, churches, and schools, connected with three, not one, railroads and a waterfront on the Columbia River whistling with commerce. Only later did the midwesterners who bought lots in Cascade City off the plat map discover that the townsite at Section 1, Township 16, Range 32, was only a torrid spot on the prairie above Providence Coulee, 60 miles short of the Columbia. Cascade City is part of Washington's silhouette.

A better boomer was Francis H. Cook. Cook founded the *Tacoma Herald*, Tacoma's first paper, but in 1879, he followed the eastern tide of Washington endeavor and shipped his press to Spokane. There, on Independence Day 1879 Cook editorialized in his *Spokan* (he would forever drop the final e) *Times*:

> *There is probably no country now known to the American people, the name of which sounds so pleasantly upon the ear of the homeless and unsettled, as that of Northeastern Washington. Man has scarcely dreamed, in his most extravagant fancies, of an ideal country which has not a counterpart in the vicinity of Spokan . . . We would gratify his curiosity. Here he may ascend to a dizzy mountain height and look admiringly down upon the beautiful and the grand.*

Aside from the fact that the mountains around Spokane are not especially vertiginous, Cook's "beautiful and the grand" is the formula for the sublime effects of Washington's topography. It's the mountains. Old American settings along the Hudson River and beside the Adirondacks are picturesque. Here they are also grand.

Washington took the final outline of its profile in 1863 when Idaho Territory was separated from it. Idaho's peculiar panhandle was ultimately drawn not by Boise's desire for a land bridge to Canada but by Olympia's anxieties that Eastern Washington, swelling then with prospectors and soon wheat ranchers, would want to move the territorial capitol from Budd Inlet to Walla Walla. Francis Cook was one of the majority in eastern Washington and northern Idaho who wanted to reunite the two mostly Republican territories at the panhandle. Twice, in 1878 and again in 1887, the union was advanced and both times beaten back, on the last occasion by Democrat President Grover Cleveland's pocket veto of an annexation bill that had passed both branches of Congress.

Actually, Idaho is much older than Washington. As you travel west from the Rocky Mountains, the land gets younger. The Olympics are the youngest. The creation of Idaho's seaport with the completion of the slackwater Snake River to Lewiston in 1975 may be considered a resumption of its destiny. About 300 million years ago, the future border between Idaho's panhandle and Washington state was on the Pacific coast.

Washington has a wet side and a dry side. Drawing the border between them is not so easy. Since the heavy rains spill over the ceiling of the Cascades, the moist and the arid are not evenly divided by the Pacific Crest. You can sense the changes that occur between the dripping and dry climates by driving east of Snoqualmie Pass. The vegetation proceeds from Douglas-fir through western larch, lodgepole pine, ponderosa pine, willow, black cottonwood, sagebrush, and blue bunch wheatgrass. One can imagine a meteorological border zigzagging through the band of western larch, where the mingling of rain and sunlight regularly bridges the state's two parts with extravagant rainbows. Often the politics passing between the state's two sides is even more colorful.

Lake Chelan is another gauge of the changes that occur between the state's wet and dry sides. The fifty-mile cruise from Lake Chelan to Stehekin is also the most relaxing way to penetrate the North Cascades. Cascade Crest is only another fifteen impassable miles due west. Or, over a less direct route by road and trail, it is thirty miles to Cascade Pass.

Judging by photographs, the best spot in Washington to catch a rainbow is Palouse Falls, five miles north of the Snake River on the border between Whitman and Franklin counties. The rainbows there can be a palliative for the falls themselves, which are sometimes brown with the silt of fertile Palouse soil. The twisted course and behavior of the Palouse River are more evidence that the fluid dynamics of the state's dry flank are as surprising as its wet. Before the Army Corps of Engineers "channelized" the Palouse through Pullman and Colfax, the river would periodically carry parts of those communities away in flash floods. Walla Walla's Mill Creek was another carefree flooder until it was

A windmill at sunset in the Palouse. ART WOLFE.

disciplined by the Army Corps. "Walla Walla," of course, means many waters.

Pullman's pioneers were especially proud of their bubbling artesian well in the town center, and sketches of it figured prominently in their self-promotions. Their self-respect ascended suddenly when the state legislature awarded the town the state agricultural college, now Washington State University. There are more than eight hundred artesian wells in the state, and many of them spout from aquifers on its eastern half. The freshwater-challenged San Juan Islands have not been so lucky.

For more fresh water surprises, you may submerge in Spokane. After years of struggling to keep the Spokane River suitable for drawing domestic water, the city water department discovered in 1907 that Spokane sat on top of an ancient underground river of immense volume. The Spokane-Rathdrum Aquifer was rapidly developed into the community's sole source of fresh— and very hard—water. Spokane's environs are wet on the surface as well. Like everyone else who grew up there, I memorized the Spokane Chamber of Commerce's principal advertisement for summer fun in the area—"fifty lakes within fifty miles and one hundred lakes within a hundred miles."

For three hundred miles between the Spokane and Snake Rivers, there are no significant tributaries feeding the Columbia River from the east. This is the Big Bend, the driest part of the state's dry side, defined by the great 300-mile semi-circle the Columbia wraps around it.

The best panoramic portrait of the Big Bend's greening is in red from an altitude of 570 miles. The Landsat satellite's infrared aerial views reveal the Columbia Basin irrigation project dappled with burgundy rectangles and vivid red dots. The wide circles of the latter are drawn by center pivot irrigation. The cool blue aridity of channeled scablands, coulees, ridges, and plateaus encroaches from every direction but does not dominate. Just south of the project, and below the chin of the river's Big Bend profile, the Department of Energy's

Hanford Reservation is a cyanogen blue dusted by the lighter turquoise of the sand dunes piling up across the river from Ringold. At Ringold, on the east side of the river, the project is met again in the Big Bend's neck. The Landsat's red and blue portrait is also a perfect gauge of how the rains increase as the weather moves east across the Palouse. There the unirrigated wheat lands are nearly as ruddy as the bean, onion, potato, alfalfa, hay, and beet fields of the irrigated basin.

The irrigation of the Big Bend repeats in the controlled flow of its 2,300 miles of canals what the receding Ice Age did in an apocalyptic flood—or floods. Compared to Idaho's claim for an ancient seashore, this is very recent history—only a few thousand years old. The story of these late-Pleistocene cataclysms is calculated to excite the imaginations of Washington eighth graders obliged to study state history. The story is also graphically told with a variety of multi-media aids at Dry Falls State Park visitors' center. At four hundred feet high and nearly four miles wide, Dry Falls was probably the world's greatest waterfall. These effects came suddenly, not from the inch-by-inch receding of glaciers, but from abrupt breaks in huge ice dams releasing periodic floods that were many times the combined flows of all the world's rivers. The Big Bend's strange and unique scablands are the result of scouring by these floods.

Washington has rain belts, sun belts, banana belts, and micro-climates so specialized that in places you can walk just a mile and feel the difference. Especially on the wet side of the Cascades, you can enjoy the subtleties of the temperate zone. The Olympic Peninsula is a microcosm of climates which, although they may vary dramatically, are usually gentle. Drive west from the sun belt of Sequim to the rain forests of the Hoh River valley and every mile you motor you can expect on the average more than an additional inch of precipitation annually. The water temperatures of Puget Sound also vary markedly. When the Puget lobe of the Pleistocene glaciation withdrew its lid, hundreds of miles of irregular shoreline were exposed. Since then, a few thousand years of silting from the sound's many tributaries have created shallows which the tides alternately inundate and expose. Here, on hot summer days when they ebb, the sands bake. And when the tides return, they bring with them a bathtub for swimmers. The tidelands beach I'm most familiar with is on Samish Bay at the south end of Chuckanut Drive. A few miles south, the shore birds of Padilla Bay are delighted year round by the eelgrass beds that grow on the mud flats there. You can swim there as well, sharing the tub with other summer visitors like sandpipers, killdeers, winged teals, gulls galore, and common snipes.

Speaking of bathtubs, Puget Sound itself is something of one. At Admiralty Inlet, its entrance off Port Townsend, the sound is considerably shallower than it is, for instance, off Seattle's Magnolia Bluff where the West Point outfall releases treated sewage from the Metro treatment plant. So Puget Sound is not the great self-flusher it was once thought to be. Its deepest waters are a pool for the heavier pollutants that Tacoma, Seattle, and Everett supply. Of course, those waters are much too cold for swimmers—but not for bottom fish.

There is in Washington a long and pleasing history of swords being beaten into plowshares. Because, historically the military often took the best ground, the return of sites, like most of Fort Lawton for Seattle's Discovery Park and the runways and Lake Washington shoreline of Sandpoint Naval Station for Warren G. Magnuson Park, represents victories for the culture of recreation and imagination. Another liberation is the highest point on Vashon Island, where an abandoned Niki Missile site has been developed into a field of dreams for the island's little leaguers.

A number of state parks are also the peaceful result of military plans. Those at Forts Worden, Casey, and Flagler formed a triangle for blasting targets on Admiralty Inlet from three directions. Built at the turn of the century largely to defend the Navy Shipyard at Bremerton against the attack of another Spanish Armada, the trio never fired a shot in anger. Now these old forts and their concrete bunkers are among the state's most favored attractions.

For nearly a century the Puget Sound Naval Shipyard at Bremerton has been an attraction primarily because its battleships were a scenic hour's ferry ride from Seattle. However, the U.S.S. *Missouri*, World War II's "Mighty Mo" and long the yard's principal lure, after a tour of duty in the Gulf War, was deactivated in 1992 and left Puget Sound. The most famous historical vessel to regularly make the round trip between the yard and Seattle was the silver teardrop-shaped *Kalakala* which at its commission in 1935, was called by its promoter, Captain Peabody of the Black Ball Line, the "World's first streamlined ferry." Until the construction of the Space Needle for the Century 21 World's Fair in 1962, the *Kalakala* was probably the most widely known symbol of the Puget Sound area.

In the old Chinook trade talk, *Kalakala* means "flying bird." Throughout the history of Puget Sound's "Mosquito Fleet" steamers and its car ferries, many have been given native names. Some names are shared. When the *Elwha* was built in 1967, it was one of the class of Superferries, then the largest ever built to operate on Puget Sound. A Quillayute word meaning "elk," Elwha is also the name of a town, river, mountain range, and reservoir, all in Clallam County.

Certainly, while giving some historical resonance to the features of Washington's portrait, we need to consider those marks which Washingtonians have added to the landscape as well as those we found here. For this, we may return to my old home neighborhood on Ninth Avenue and its dead end and look west into the Big Bend. The panorama there still plays for me like a piano roll of an enchanting old tune with every feature striking a familiar note. But there have been changes. The graceful arpeggios of the Hangman Creek Bridge's monumental concrete arches are hidden behind the architectural noise of the new and merely functional I-90 bridge beside it. This is a modern lament.

With a few heartening exceptions, Washington's civic architecture of the last fifty years is dismal when compared to what was built earlier. About the time the Dorpats moved to Washington, newcomers and descendants of early residents increasingly forsook their parents' progressive efforts. Rather than ennoble their communities with distinguished landmarks, they settled instead for scaled-down structures that seemed modeled after warehouses, portables, and gaudy roadside attractions. Spokane's distinguished Classic Revival post office (1909) can barely withstand the discomfort of the

modern federal building built beside it in 1967. Both Seattle's and King County's modern municipal buildings are tedious monuments to mediocrity. The seat of Seattle city government resembles a hotel-motel—a cheap one.

Thankfully, there are survivors of our grand old ways. The Whatcom Museum of History and Art is housed in one of the state's best examples of late Victorian civic architecture. Perhaps in need of room, Bellingham's municipal offices were moved in 1940 from this "most photographed structure in Washington" to new quarters. Unfortunately, the replacement resembles a bunker more than a distinguished seat of city government. However, the eminent county courthouses in Pomeroy, Montesano, and Port Townsend survive and continue to be used as centers of government. Since the early 1970s, there has been an impressive proliferation of heritage groups statewide— historical societies, museums, and municipal libraries with history rooms. Encouraged and stimulated by both the country's bi-centennial in 1976 and the state's centennial in 1989, these activists, for the most part volunteers, have saved and restored dozens of distinguished landmarks that might otherwise have been sacrificed to the bottom-line pieties of performance and profit. The recent restoration of Columbia County's elegant courthouse in Dayton is especially satisfying.

The Spokane County courthouse is one of the jewels of state architecture. Upstream from this monumental chateau is Riverfront Park, the site of the 1974 World's Fair. The park is landscaped around a network of pools and islands linked by the handsome bridges across the Spokane River. The best of the fair structures have been saved, notably the Opera House and the clock tower of the old Great Northern depot. And all is serenaded by Spokane Falls babbling in antiphony with piped music rolling from the park's restored carousel. As a child I rode its colorful hand-carved horses and chased its golden rings when this venerable amusement was still at Spokane's old Natatorium Park. A climb from the carousel at Riverfront Park through downtown to another ring, the basalt mound of Cliff Park on South Hill, requires about as much rambling as a trek around Seattle's Green Lake. Or a walk from Esther Short Park to the Vancouver Barracks by way of Saint James Church and Vancouver's Carnegie Library. Or a stroll from Tacoma's Old City Hall to the Washington State Historical Society's Ferry Museum by way of the Wright Park conservatory and Stadium High. These are a few of Washington's many revealing community rambles.

The state's several campuses preserve some of its best architecture. The University of Washington campus, the most distinguished collection of public buildings in the state, is recognized far beyond the state border for its extraordinary setting. At the southeast corner of campus, the university's academic Gothic theme is repeated in one of the state's most distinguished bridges. The Montlake Bascule Bridge crosses the Lake Washington Ship Canal's narrowest cut, and it is a short walk from its southern end to the Museum of History and Industry, the Waterfront Nature Trail, and the University of Washington Arboretum. Walk-abouts on state campuses at Pullman, Ellensburg, and Bellingham are also intellectually enlivening for visitors and students alike.

The golfers of Washington are also blessed with fairways that can ameliorate the strain of the game. Of the many municipal golf courses in the state which merit their green fees, Spokane's Indian Canyon seems to me especially worth the humiliation that its hills, ravines, and deep roughs will add to your handicap, simply for the setting and the views it extends beyond the Spokane River valley to Mount Spokane.

When traveling to Portland from Spokane, Dad would often turn the pointed nose of the family's aerodynamic late-1940s Studebaker (our first new car in Washington) on a detour to State Highway 97. Climbing south out of Toppenish and the Yakima Valley, there was a good chance of seeing wild horses running the ridges of Horse Heaven Hills. The next attraction was Goldendale. Nearby is a highland from which the necklace of Cascade volcanoes—Mounts Rainier, Adams, Hood, and Jefferson and the Three Sisters—can be seen in one grand panorama.

Morning sun on golden cottonwoods reflects in the still waters of the Wenatchee River. TERRY DONNELLY.

For us, Goldendale had a second and equal attraction: the water. We would drink up and parody dad's insistence that it was the best water in Washington by letting quantities dribble down our chins and splash our collars. It was refreshing. From Goldendale the quick descent to the Columbia Gorge is interrupted by two of Sam Hill's many concretions: Maryhill and Stonehenge.

Sam Hill was Washington's charismatic of concrete. He envisioned and fought for highways tying the communities and culture of Washington together. And when he felt his adopted state was in need of it, he imported culture. Maryhill, the concrete chateau he originally planned for his home, Hill named for his wife. Instead it was dedicated a museum in 1926 by his friend, Queen Marie of Romania. Stonehenge, three miles east of Maryhill, is Sam Hill's replica of the British original kitschfully restored to its prehistoric splendor with reinforced concrete. Now it's something of a mecca—or "power place"—for New Age druids, especially at times of lunar eclipse.

But highways were Sam Hill's first obsession. Construction of the state's early-century system was largely due to the lobbying of his Good Roads Association. The Peace Arch at Blaine—again, built of concrete with bronze doors bolted always open—was financed by a combination of Hill's dollars and pennies collected by school children in Washington and British Columbia. "Children of a Common Mother" is the piece of Anglophilia inscribed on the U.S. side of this monument to an undefended border. But the arch is also a heroic memorial to the Pacific Highway and all the other state roads that Hill and his highwaymen promoted and saw built. Long before he got on the go with roads, Sam married Mary, the eldest daughter of the Great Northern Railway's "Empire Builder," James J. Hill. And therein lies an irony of transportation effects. Sam Hill was too good at building highways. Ultimately, he helped steal the hearts and minds of Washingtonians away from the railroads and so also from what rails can do best. If you climb to the summit of Mount Si, you get the picture. Except on the coldest or windiest days, the view west towards Seattle is fouled by the smog shrouds that cover the freeways. Now to help clear

the air we are importing Europe again—Spanish trains that hurry passengers between Portland and Seattle and soon, we hope, through Blaine, passing just below Hill's arch, to British Columbia.

Christened on March 19, 1825, with the swing of a bottle of rum against a flag post supporting the Union Jack, the Hudson's Bay Company's Fort Vancouver was named for the first European expedition to explore upstream from the Columbia's dangerous bar at its mouth. The first, however, to cross the bar was not the English captain but a Boston merchant named Robert Gray, and the name of his ship was *Columbia.*

Both Gray and Vancouver visited the river in 1792. Gray told Vancouver where to find it. Thirteen years later in 1805, the Lewis and Clark expedition made it by land to the mouth of the river. Beacon Rock is among the many features that the American explorers named. A switch-back trail leads less than a mile to its 850-foot summit. From there one understands the allusion to the river as the "Rhine of the West." The view looks east into the picturesque Columbia Gorge and west towards Portland and Vancouver. From both directions one can still imagine how the river appeared from time primordial to 1938 when, less than five miles east of Beacon Rock, the river was backed up behind Bonneville Dam.

Made miserable by winds off the Pacific, Lewis and Clark stayed only a short time on the north side of the river before they followed the advice of the local Chinook Indians and made a protected camp near the present city of Astoria, Oregon. One hundred and seventy years later, Astoria was also the destination of Marine captain Alan Jones who swam five hundred miles from the Snake River twin cities of Clarkston and Lewiston to the mouth of the Columbia. Jones did his crawl for the 1975 opening of the lock at Lower Granite Dam on the Snake River. Lower Granite was the last of eight dams that gave Idaho its seaport to the Pacific. Jones took thirty-two days to make his swim through the slackwater behind the dams. Thirteen years earlier Spence Campbell made the same swim. However, this college student from Orofino, Idaho, did it five days faster than the Marine. With only four dam pools to stroke through, Campbell was propelled along most of the Snake by its current. Unlike the patriotic Marine,

Campbell took his long plunge to earn tuition for medical school—donations mostly from the citizens of his hometown. When he stepped ashore at Astoria, he was ceremonially greeted by Oregon's governor Mark Hatfield and given a kiss from the community queen. He was not, however, met by his promoter who had absconded with the funds, leaving Spence Campbell to hitchhike home. One cruel wit advised him to swim back and spawn. Now, four Snake River dams later, it's a journey the salmon themselves find daunting. The transcontinental Northern Pacific Railroad was completed through Spokane, Cheney, Sprague, and Pasco in 1883. The "first thru train"—the name was painted on the side—to return east was filled with salmon. The sides of its twenty cars were artfully ornamented with salmon and the names of their shippers and consignees.

Since the early 1930s, when the Army Corps of Engineers recommended converting the Columbia into an irrigation ditch and power generator, eleven dams have been built across its 745 miles from the 49th parallel to the Columbia bar. Among the first public works produced in this regulation of the river was Washington's official folk song, "Roll On Columbia." Woody Guthrie composed it on his guitar in the back seat of a Bonneville Power Administration car as he was driven around the project by a BPA official. The first verse reads,

Uncle Sam took up the challenge
In the year of Thirty-Three
For the farmer and the factory
and for all of you and me,
He said, 'Roll along, Columbia,
You can ramble to the sea
But River, while you're rambling,
You can do some work for me.'

Before the rambling Columbia was put to work, its 1,284-foot descent through Washington made navigation frequently difficult for anything but the salmon. In two places—Celilo and Kettle Falls—the river was impassable even to the Indian navigators (whom Lewis and Clark described as the most skilled oarsmen they had ever encountered). Now the dams of the main stem divide this fall between them—unevenly. The drop at

Grand Coulee Dam is by far the longest: 530 feet. Only the dams below the Snake River have locks.

With Goldendale's fresh waters sustaining us, our family's Highway 97 detour to Portland dropped from Maryhill to the Columbia and our next attraction, Celilo Falls. The Indians who gathered there to net and spear salmon as they leapt the falls worked from precarious scaffolds that hung over the cataracts like Rube Goldberg contraptions. They were, of course, centuries-old and most appropriate constructions. For the Indians, the 1957 inundation of Celilo Falls behind The Dalles Dam—which also flooded a number of native funerary islands—was an especially tough hit. Above the dam near Horsethief Lake State Park is a full-faced native petroglyph whose wide eyes look down on the scene. Its native name Tsagaglalal means "She Who Watches." If we dare rate the many aspects of Washington's portrait, Tsagaglalal must be one of the most meaningful.

On May 18, 1980, at 8:32 a.m., Washington time lurched forward when one of its most picturesque creations exploded. Mount St. Helens, which had been patiently created through a few millennia of relatively constructive eruptions, forthwith blew 1,300 feet from its summit and opened its belly. Much of the ash, carried by prevailing winds, spread east across the state. The rendered north side of the mountain catapulted across Spirit Lake and flooded west into the Toutle and Cowlitz Rivers. In a matter of hours, the floor of the Columbia was covered with mud flows to a depth that effectively stopped travel on the river and stranded container ships in Vancouver and Portland.

Aside from the state's various portraits of Mount Rainier, two peaks, Mount Shuksan from the Mount Baker Highway in the North Cascades and Mount St. Helens across Spirit Lake historically received the most attention from photographers. Now they are returning to the Mount St. Helens National Volcanic Monument to shoot across the gray shores of Spirit Lake into the incision in the mountain's north side and to the lava dome that is again slowly growing there. The photographers are beginning to record what will be the long story of the mountain's recovery—from the weird and grotesque to becoming again, perhaps, the grand and dignified saint of the lower Columbia valley.

The last piece of land at the state's southwest corner is manmade land, the North Jetty that sticks out from Cape Disappointment. A hike to the end of this rocky brink exposes one to the force of the Pacific and the crashing of the Columbia bar, the "Graveyard of the Pacific." Navy Lieuteuant Charles Wilkes lost a ship here, the *Peacock*, in 1841, long before there were any buoys, the jetty, or the lighthouses at Cape Disappointment and North Head. Less than two miles apart, the two lights look south over the Columbia's mouth and north towards Long Beach respectively. Long Beach is one of the delightful creations of Washington's coastline. It's a twenty-five-mile spit that for nearly twenty of those miles separates the Pacific Ocean from the oysters of Willapa Bay and the cranberries of her bogs. Serenely protected near the southern end of this harbor, Long Island contains one of the most ancient cedar forests of the world. Individual trees are as old as 1,000 years and the grove itself much older. This gem of a so-called "climax forest" is part of the Willapa Bay National Wildlife Forest, and fortunately a visit to it requires sincere effort.

Far up the coast at Captain Cook's Cape Flattery, the lighthouse stands offshore on Tatoosh Island, the westernmost part of the contiguous forty-eight states and Washington's northwest corner—or one of them. Blaine at the border with British Columbia on Semiahmoo Bay is another. And for those who count stranded pieces of the 1864 boundary settlement, Point Roberts, the about-five-square-mile peninsula hanging from Canada into the Strait of Georgia, is a third. Traditionally, Point Roberts was the watering hole for dry Canadians before they revoked their blue Sundays.

Cape Flattery and Tatoosh Island are part of the Makah Reservation. Tatoosh—or Tu-tutsh—means Thunder Bird, a Makah totem. Immediately south of the reservation is Shi Shi Beach, considered by an assortment of Washington's nature poets and waterscape artists as the most captivating spot in the state. The beach stretches for about three miles between Portage Head and the Point of Arches. Fortunately, the road to Shi Shi has been closed by the regular christening that the beach and its headlands receive from the Pacific. Now one must hike out through the reservation, following both its trail and its rule to reserve local shellfish for the Makah's use.

The next headland, Cape Alava, is about six miles south of Point of Arches. It is reached by a three-mile hike from Lake Ozette along a trail that is often supported on planks above the rain forest floor. Approaching the beach is a natural contest of sorts between the sound of the surf and the aroma of the ocean air. The beach is a favorite two-day, one-night retreat for visitors. At Cape Alava, the Ozette Village site is one of the oldest settlements in the state—about 2,000 years. Understandably, it is also one of the nation's most valued archeological digs, a work done in cooperation between the Ozettes and the archaeologists of Washington State University. Getting to the trail head at Lake Ozette is as prepossessing as hiking to the coast. The bucolic scenes of meadows, barns, farmhouses, and clumps of spreading trees, landscaped, for the most part, by Scandinavian immigrant farmers, make the road from Clallam Bay on the Strait of Juan De Fuca one of the pastoral delights of the state.

The rain forests of the Olympic Peninsula may be Washington's greatest contribution to the planet's diversity. The belt that extends from Oregon to Alaska is richest here where a wide coastline gives the weather space to stew against the Olympics and dump the hundreds of inches of rain needed to create this mattressed tangle of spruce, hemlock, ferns, and mosses. The long valleys of the Quillayute, Hoh, Queets and Quinault Rivers, especially, are fecund with these forests.

Following the Quinault beyond Lake Quinault to the river's source leads one into the interior of Olympic National Park. About eight miles beyond the road's end, the rain forest suddenly opens onto Enchanted Valley. In the distance a glaciated Mount Anderson rises above the head of the valley like an altar. Both sides of this nave are precipitous, and the north wall is baptized by waterfalls. After continuing about three miles along the valley's open floor, the trail begins its switchback ascent to Anderson Pass which is reached in a mile or so.

These four or five miles between the rain forest and the pass are my Enchantments. I've made this trek three times, but the last time, I regret to confess, is now a quarter of a century ago.

In nearly a half-century of living in Washington, I've moved from hiking into the Hangman Creek Canyon, through climbing in the Cascades and Olympics, to walking around Wallingford—the neighborhood in Seattle where I've lived now for fourteen years. Wallingford is one of the steaming compost bins of Lesser Seattle, that loose group of ironists who promote this community by pretending to discourage people from visiting it. Those among us who cherish Washington's wild rivers, its remote mountain valleys, and its strange scablands also promote a kind of Lesser Washington state-of-consciousness. Thus, although it hurts to limit the number of hikers who can visit the Alpine Lakes Wilderness Area each year, the million who hiked the Cascades between Snoqualmie and Stevens Passes last year often hurt those high wild lands more. Now we must wait in line, for in the Enchantments less ultimately means more. Again, stay on the trail.

Not long ago a group of old Washington rock 'n' rollers campaigned to change the state anthem from the corny old hat, "Washington My Home," to the internationally known rock anthem, "Louie, Louie." Composed in the mid-1950s and played by the Kingsmen, a Washington band which still rocks about the state, the lyrics read in part:

Louie Louie, Me Gotta Go,
Ya Ya Ya Ya Ya Ya.

Since no one could explain why whoever was leaving Louie for whatever reason had anything to do with Washington, the song's original lyricist, Richard Berry, in a fit of state patriotism added this quatrain for the campaign:

Louie Louie, Me Gotta Go,
I get a call from Washington
To the Northwest I must come
To sing the song everybody knows.

This tongue-in-cheek attempt to have a Washington-born classic of rock 'n roll stamped with the state's official imprimatur was a popular gag. It shows that Washington state's portrait is smiling.

Or, for more laughs, visit George, Washington. Here's a bit of playfulness with state identity that Washington school children would understand—however, not as parody. Although the streets are named for varieties of cherry trees and the locals occasionally dress up in revolutionary costumes, George, Washington, does not rival Williamsburg, Virginia, for colonial authenticity.

George is near the Gorge, an improved natural amphitheater that looks across the Columbia River into the setting sun. This venue for popular music attracts fans from throughout Washington because it is near the center of the state. But how should we calculate the very center of Washington? If we draw intersecting lines from four of the state's five corners—choosing Cape Flattery over Blaine for the point of northwest origin—the lines meet, surprisingly, a few miles east of Snoqualmie Pass. This is about where the western larch takes over from the Douglas-fir, or near where we earlier drew the meander line separating the state's dry and wet sides.

Or consider Washington's place in the Union—at its center. Once considered the backside of America, since statehood came to Hawaii and Alaska, we are very near the heart of it. More importantly, Washington state is on the Pacific Rim. Easily, the most gratifying development is the increased presence of Asian influences here. The trade—which began with Captain Cook's innocent choice of north coast sea otter furs to soften the mattresses of his crew and which soon became a mercantile sensation when it was discovered that the otter pelts were considered essential trimming for the costumes of Chinese courtiers—is now busy with all manner of hard and soft stuff. And much of it is made in Washington, including, of course, Boeing jets. There is even some evidence from artifacts found along the coast that the first non-natives to visit here were Asians, who preceded Cook's voyage, perhaps by centuries. In 1834 the sailing vessel Llama, which brought three milk cows and a bull from California to Fort Nisqually, also carried shipwrecked Japanese who were picked up near Cape

Flattery. The reality of Washington state's centrality to both the Union and this Asian energy suggests, perhaps, that some town in Washington, I nominate George, be considered as America's next capital city. That is, in the eventuality that the first wears out or becomes too remote. The additional plats required could be lined with streets named for eastern cities and other exotic Americana.

But perhaps we make too much here of geopolitics. Finally it will not be Washington's politicians or its products that will be remembered, but its mountains and its art. That, hopefully, is what you will receive from this book: an alliance of art and nature. *Washington: A Portrait of the Evergreen State* may be seen as of a genre with the Indian petroglyphs that have been carved, stained, and preserved on the state's basalt and granite tablets. They are Washington's oldest testament. This, its most recent.

Years hence it may be possible to visit a Washington State Theme Park. There will be virtual-reality bald eagle flights over the Cascades, salmon journeys in and out of spawning grounds, and rides over both Dry Falls and Snoqualmie Falls before they were diverted or dried up. Then one will be able to swim to speed with the orca whales in Puget Sound, tour an old growth forest on the wing of a spotted owl, and safely ride the original Tacoma Narrows Bridge as it gallops and falls into Puget Sound. Then, also, everyone will be able to climb Mount Rainier, by any route, and spend the night on top communicating with the Old Man in the Crater. I'd gladly climb on any of those rides.

But future Washingtonians should also be able to actually walk in the woods, approach Mount Adams from the Yakima Valley when the fall colors set the aspens ablaze, ride the low road through the Yakima River Canyon between Ellensburg and Yakima, float on top of Soap Lake, drink coffee and stay sleepless in Seattle, attend a strawberry festival—somewhere, browse the stacks of Whitman College's Penrose Library, paddle an inner-tube out on Moses Lake, climb Mount Bonaparte, ride the rapids of the Lewis River, buy a fresh salmon at Seattle's Pike Place Market, and read about Sasquatches but never run into one.

E. S. Ingraham apparently never returned to visit with his Sub-Rainian apparition in the steam caves atop Mount Rainier. However, the Old Man of the Crater is surely a variation of our popular legend, the shy Sasquatch, the largest of the state totems that doesn't swim. I believe there is only one way to approach these demure and delicate chimeras, the Sub-Rainian and the Sasquatch—as poetic go-betweens. Through their eternal wanderings, Washington's past meets its future. In other words—consider this the moral—the popular Sasquatch is a mythopoeic test of our own attitudes and affections. If Washingtonians continue to treat the Big Foot kindly and preserve for it a private place in their enchantments, *this Washington* will step lightly into the future.

Paul Dorpat
Seattle, 1994

"*Especially on a late summer evening, Seattle's modern skyscape can put on a show. The glow of a northern sunset and the lights of the freeway reflect against the glass, steel, and polymer curtains of the central business district. It is not an Emerald City then. The many colors scattered from the skyline resemble a diadem and suggest the name 'Queen City.'*"

PAUL DORPAT

22

As seen from Rizal Park, the Seattle skyline aglow.   TERRY DONNELLY.

Downtown Seattle, with the Pike Place Market in the foreground.   TERRY DONNELLY.

One of Seattle's many espresso bars, Pioneer Square.   BRUCE HANDS.

Buying fruits and vegetables at Seattle's Pike Place Market.   TOM AND PAT LEESON.

Historic Pioneer Square in downtown Seattle reflects many cultures.   TERRY DONNELLY.

A teahouse and brightly colored Japanese maples in the Japanese Garden, Washington Park Arboretum, Seattle.   TERRY DONNELLY.

Houseboats on Seattle's Lake Union.   TERRY DONNELLY.

Magnolias in bloom at the Volunteer
Park Conservatory, Seattle.   ESTHER THOMPSON.

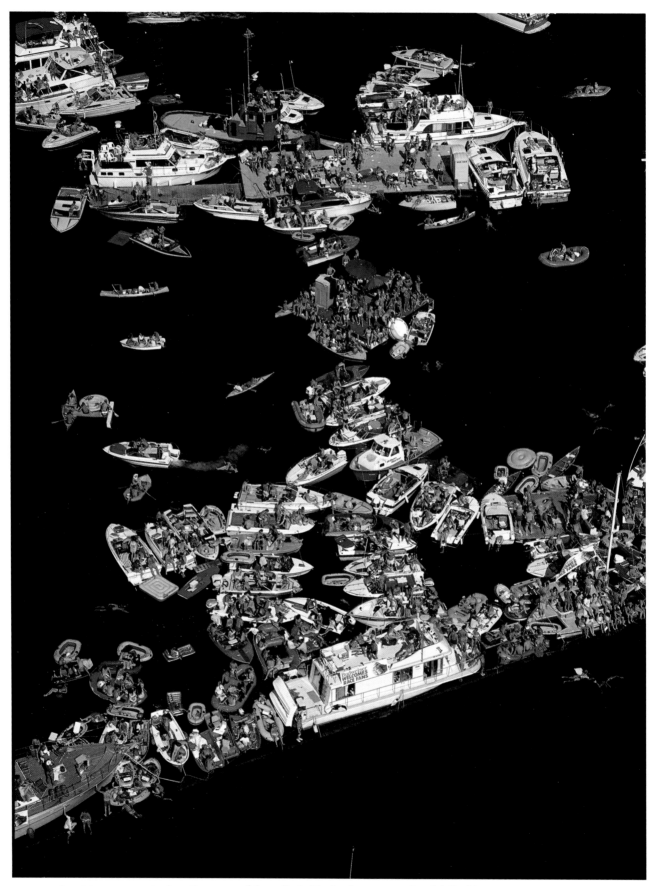

Spectators congregate along the course of the unlimited hydroplane races at Seattle's Seafair.   MARTY LOKEN/ALLSTOCK.

A commercial fisherman on Lake Union, Seattle. BRUCE HANDS.

Seattle's Space Needle at night. CURT GIVEN.

Building 767 jets at Boeing's Everett plant. TOM AND PAT LEESON.

"It [the main trait of Seattle's people] is a combination of energy, determination, and optimism—a trait that has made Seattle famous."

L. BYRD MOCK
The Seattle Spirit, 1911

The facade of Suzzallo Library at dusk, University of Washington, Seattle.   TERRY DONNELLY.

"*The University of Washington campus, the most distinguished collection of public buildings in the state, is recognized far beyond the state border for its extraordinary setting.*"

PAUL DORPAT

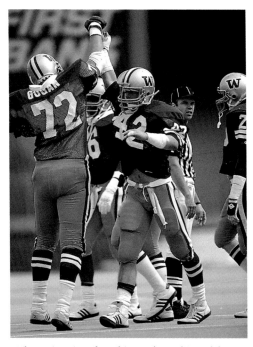

The University of Washington's Huskies celebrate.
BRIAN DRAKE.

Husky Stadium at the University of Washington during a game.   WAYNE BARTZ/ALLSTOCK.

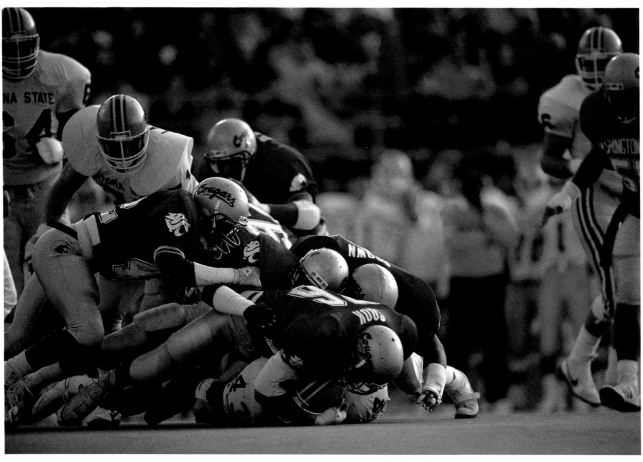

The Washington State Cougars take down an opposing ball carrier.   BRIAN DRAKE.

Seattle's semi-pro hockey team, the Thunderbirds.   BRIAN DRAKE.

The Seattle Seahawks show winning form.   BRIAN DRAKE.

Forward Shawn Kemp scores for the Seattle Supersonics.   BRIAN DRAKE.

On a September morning, wildflowers decorate Norway Pass Overlook, Mount St. Helens and Spirit Lake in the background.   JEFF GNASS.

The dramatic crater of Washington's most active volcano, Mount St. Helens.   DAVID FALCONER/F-STOCK.

"*On May 18, 1980, at 8:32 a.m., Washington time lurched forward when one of its most picturesque creations exploded. Mount St. Helens, which had been patiently created through a few millenia of relatively constructive eruptions, forthwith blew 1,300 feet from its summit and opened its belly.*"

PAUL DORPAT

Water droplets on a tiger lily, Kaniksu National Forest.   SCOTT PRICE.

Mount Adams is Washington's second highest peak.   RUSSELL LAMB.

Sunrise colors the south face of Mount Rainier.   CHARLES GURCHE.

Climbers heading for Camp Muir on Mount Rainier.   CLIFF LIGHT.

" *I saw from my home thousands of sunsets over . . . Mount Rainier, [its] glaciers tinged with red or gold as if some artist of Paul Bunyan proportions were using [its] ice fields as his canvas.* "

WILLIAM O. DOUGLAS
Of Men and Mountains, 1950

Llamas and hikers switchback down the Pacific Crest Trail,
Mount Adams Wilderness.   BRUCE HANDS.

White and pink heather, with Mount Challenger and Whatcom Peak in the background, North Cascades National Park. PAT O'HARA.

Mount Baker Wilderness in winter white. PAT O'HARA.

On Mount Baker, a climber enjoys the morning sun.   JON GNASS.

The Columbia white-tailed deer is an endangered species.   TOM AND PAT LEESON.

" *Every part of this country is sacred to my people. Every hillside, every valley, every plain and grove has been hallowed by some fond memory or sad experience of my tribe.* "

CHIEF SEATTLE, 1887

The Carbon River carves its gorge near the entrance to Mount Rainier National Park. PAT O'HARA.

Rugged Prusik Peak stands 8,200 feet above sea level in Mount Baker National Forest. RUSSELL LAMB.

A backpacker gazes into Crystal Lake, Alpine Lakes Wilderness.   DAVE SCHIEFELBEIN.

Western larch in fall, Colville National Forest.   SCOTT PRICE.

A convoy of log trucks waits to unload at a log dump near Hoquiam.   TOM AND PAT LEESON.

Preparing raw logs for export, Port of Olympia.   BRUCE HANDS.

"*One of the most awesome sights of the primordial American continent must have been the great stands of virgin timber in the Pacific Northwest . . . rolling blankets of Douglas fir laid across the land, some of the trees as high as 280 feet, interspersed with hemlock and cedar, and then, on the eastern slope, millions of ponderosa pine, aspen, and cottonwood.*"

NEIL R. PEIRCE
The Pacific States of America, 1972

A summer evening light show illuminates the spillway at Grand Coulee Dam.   TOM AND PAT LEESON.

" *The morning fog lifts like a curtain in the granite canyon of the Columbia River and reveals the most massive concrete escarpment in the world, stretching from cliff to cliff. It is nearly a mile long and as thick as two city blocks. At the base its bulk is three times that of the Great Pyramid; it contains enough concrete to pave a roadway around the globe. This is the Grand Coulee Dam.* "

RICHARD NEUBERGER
"Miracle in Concrete"
The Nation, June 1, 1940

The Washington State Capitol Building, Olympia.   PAT O'HARA.

Downtown Spokane seen across the Spokane River.   SCOTT SPIKER/F-STOCK.

Spokane's Riverfront Park, site of the 1974 World's Fair, Expo '74.   TOM AND PAT LEESON.

Our Lady of Lourdes Church, Spokane.   ESTHER E. THOMPSON.

" *R*iverfront Park . . . is landscaped around a network of pools and
islands linked by the handsome bridges across the Spokane River. . . .
And all is serenaded by Spokane Falls babbling in antiphony with
piped music from the park's restored carousel.*"*

PAUL DORPAT

Apple trees in blossom, eastern Washington.   DAVE SCHIEFELBEIN.

A worker picks apples in an eastern Washington orchard.   PAT AND TOM LEESON.

Combining the old-fashioned way, with horse power.   TOM AND PAT LEESON.

" *The serenity of the climate [of what is now Washington], the innumerable pleasing landscapes, and the abundant fertility that unassisted nature puts forth, require only . . . the industry of man . . . to render it the most lovely country that can be imagined.* "

GEORGE VANCOUVER, EXPLORER,
quoted by Edmund S. Meany
Vancouver's Discovery of Puget Sound, 1949

An old barn in a sea of wheat, eastern Washington.   DAVE SCHIEFELBEIN.

The rich grain fields of eastern Washington's Palouse region.   TOM AND PAT LEESON.

The Hot Air Balloon Stampede, Walla Walla.   DEBI OTTINGER.

Wheat and canola thrive in eastern Washington's fertile topsoil. DAVE SCHIEFELBEIN.

"The view [of the patchwork of rolling Palouse wheat fields] is variously enchanting depending on the season—a green embroidery in spring, a golden quilt at harvest, and in winter a tracery of snow and stubble."

PAUL DORPAT

Showing off freshly picked white wine grapes, Yakima Valley.   BRUCE HANDS.

The annual Mount Baker Vineyards
Grape Stomp.   BRUCE HANDS.

A cattle drive near Mazama.   BRUCE HANDS.

The auctioneer takes a bid at an eastern
Washington livestock sale.   BRUCE HANDS.

Flower growers cultivate some 1,500 acres of tulips, daffodils, and irises in northwestern Washington's Skagit Valley.   SUSAN ALWORTH.

Harvesting tulips in the Skagit Valley. ESTHER E. THOMPSON.

"*As the loggers cut eastward into the foothills, they exposed bottomlands with topsoil deeper than a tall Swede's shoulders. The farmers followed and cultivated a culture of peas, beans, corn, and tulips. Today, tourists, many on bikes, pursue the tulips.*"

PAUL DORPAT

Rainbow Bridge and its reflection, La Conner. STEVE TERRILL.

A ferry pulls in at the dock, Friday Harbor, San Juan Island.   RICK SCHAFER.

Orcas and sailboat.   TOM AND PAT LEESON.

Sea kayakers off Orcas Island, San Juan Islands.   BRUCE HANDS.

Pleasure boats at Friday Harbor, San Juan Island.   TOM AND PAT LEESON.

Owner of a sea farm, with freshly harvested oysters,
San Juan Island.   BRUCE HANDS.

The Cape Disappointment lighthouse guards the Columbia River bar and the southern Washington coast. RAY ATKESON.

Sheep graze on Whidbey Island, near Langley.   TERRY DONNELLY.

"*In these Washington wilds, living alone, all sorts of men may perchance be found—poets, philosophers, even full-blown transcendentalists, though you may go far to find them.*"

JOHN MUIR, 1889

Canoeists enjoy a quiet moment, Orcas Island.   BRUCE HANDS.

A pair of Dungeness crabs.   TOM AND PAT LEESON.

The annual canoe races, Lummi Indian Stommish Water Festival.   BRUCE HANDS.

Makah Indian girl with baking salmon at Makah Days,
Neah Bay.   TOM AND PAT LEESON

A pair of orcas at play off the Washington coast.   TOM AND PAT LEESON.

Lime Kiln Lighthouse at dusk, Haro Strait, Lime Kiln Point State Park, San Juan Island.   JEFF GNASS.

Spruce trees frame a vista along southwestern Washington's Long Beach Peninsula,
one of the longest beaches in the world.   RAY ATKESON.

" *The wildest, the most remote, and I think, the most picturesque beach area of our whole coastline lies under a pounding surf along the Pacific Ocean in the state of Washington.* "

WILLIAM O. DOUGLAS
My Wilderness:
The Pacific West, 1960

A mountain biker admires the sunset from Blue Mountain, just outside Olympic National Park. PAT O'HARA.

" *As the sun slides westward over Puget Sound, it gradually sinks behind the jagged Olympic Mountains, turning the mountains and water a portentous purple and the sky above them a flaming orange. It is a setting worthy of the final act of* Götterdammerung. "

PATRICK DOUGLAS
Saturday Review
August 21, 1976

Olympic National Park at sunset.   ART WOLFE.

Moss-covered bigleaf maples in the Hoh Rain Forest, Olympic National Park.   CHARLES GURCHE.

California quail, Olympic National Park.   ART WOLFE.

"*The rain forests of the Olympic Peninsula may be Washington's greatest contribution to the planet's diversity. The belt that extends from Oregon to Alaska is richest here where a wide coastline gives the weather space to stew against the Olympics and dump the hundreds of inches of rain needed to create this mattressed tangle of spruce, hemlock, ferns, and mosses.*"

PAUL DORPAT

Sword ferns and native rhododendrons on Mount Walker, Olympic National Park.   PAT O'HARA.

A family explores an old-growth forest, western Washington.   TOM AND PAT LEESON.

From a wooden bridge spanning the Soleduck River, hikers admire the view.   PAT O'HARA.

A bull Roosevelt elk, Olympic National Park.   CURT GIVEN.

"*T*he Olympic forests are what you imagined virgin forests were when you were as a child. They are as tall as trees of fairy tale, and dense as that. They are set deep, deep in ancient moss, damp feathery sphagnum that looks as if it went back to the beginning of time. . . . If this is the primeval forest, then nothing I ever saw before remotely deserves the name.*"*

DONALD CULROSS PEATTIE
"The Nature of Things,"
Audubon Magazine, 1941

The Elwah Valley in winter, from Hurricane Ridge, Olympic National Park.   ART WOLFE.

The lighthouse at Fort Worden State Park, Port Townsend, Mount Baker in the background.   PAT O'HARA.

Historic downtown Port Townsend.   BRUCE HANDS.

A bagpiper at the Scottish Highlands Games, Ferndale.   BRUCE HANDS.

The Tacoma Narrows Bridge with Mount Rainier in the distance.   PAT O'HARA.

"*In wintertime one would naturally expect at Tacoma the climate of the Arctic Circle, but the geographical position is here at fault, at least so far as practical results are concerned. Were there no such thing as the warm current of Japan beating against the Pacific coast, the chief winter feature here would be the ice palace. As a result Tacoma has more rain than snow. Much of the rain in Tacoma is little more than a sort of Scotch mist and people get accustomed to that sort of thing in time.*"

Harper's Weekly,
June 29, 1891

The mural on Roslyn's Cafe, Rosyln, home of the TV hit, *Northern Exposure.*   STEVE TERRILL.

Leavenworth is noted for its charming
Bavarian-style architecture.   BRUCE HANDS.

Fort Vancouver National Historic Site. JEFF GNASS.

Charter fishing boats at dock, Ilwaco Harbor, southwestern Washington.   BRUCE HANDS.

A happy fisherman and his whopper salmon,
Columbia River.   BRUCE HANDS.

Overlooking the Columbia River Gorge, the Maryhill Museum of Art houses an important collection of works by French sculptor Auguste Rodin.   STEVE TERRILL.

"*Looking fully as ancient when I first saw it was the immense pile of concrete and stone called Maryhill Castle, set high in the vast nothingness of a stark hill overlooking the Columbia's gorge.*"

STEWART H. HOLBROOK
Far Corner, 1952

Built near the Maryhill Museum, this replica of Stonehenge was the first memorial to World War I in the U.S.   STEVE TERRILL.

The "She Who Watches" petroglyph near Horsethief Lake State Park.   PAT O'HARA.

Prairie falcon, Columbia Plateau.   ART WOLFE.

" In the beginning only spoken, the native names reveal our ancient
faces. Spokane means 'children of the sun'; Cathlamet means 'stone'
for the Columbia's rocky Cathlamet Channel; Chelan, 'deep water';
Humptulips, for the river which is 'hard to pole'; and so on and on. "

PAUL DORPAT

Competitors in one of the many windsurfing competitions in the Columbia Gorge. BRUCE HANDS.

"*W*ashington's first boomers . . . emphasized the salubrious ease of this
place, the gentle rains, its freedom from malaria, the bountiful game,
and its great river, the 'River of the West'—the mighty Columbia.*"*

PAUL DORPAT

Near Stevenson, a tugboat and barge navigate the Columbia River. DAVE SCHIEFELBEIN.

Autumn colors along the Yakima River.   DAVE SCHIEFELBEIN.

A kayaker descends the Cle Elum River. PAT O'HARA.

"*The mountains of the Pacific Northwest are tangled, wild, remote, and high. They have the roar of torrents and avalanches in their throats.*"

WILLIAM O. DOUGLAS
Of Men and Mountains, 1950

Rafters on the Lewis River pause to admire Curly Creek Falls.   PAT O'HARA.

Penstemon, paintbrush, bistort, and golden pea on Silver Star Mountain, Gifford Pinchot National Forest. TOM AND PAT LEESON.

Mount Shuksan as seen from Mount Baker National Forest, North Cascade Range. RAY ATKESON.

Acknowledgments

The publisher gratefully acknowledges the following sources:

Page 3 from *Evergreen Land: A Portrait of the State of Washington* by Nard Jones. Copyright © 1947 by Dodd, Mead & Co., New York.

Page 33 from *The Seattle Spirit*, a Seattle Chamber of Commerce periodical. Published in 1911.

Page 43 from *Of Men and Mountains* by William O. Douglas. Copyright © 1950 by Harper & Brothers, New York.

Page 48 by Chief Seattle as quoted by H. A. Smith in the *Seattle Sunday Star*, November 5, 1887.

Page 53 from *The Pacific States of America* by Neal R. Peirce. Copyright © 1972 by W. W. Norton, New York.

Page 54 from "Miracle in Concrete" by Richard Neuberger. Published in *The Nation*, June 1, 1940.

Page 60 from George Vancouver as quoted by Edmond S. Meany in *Vancouver's Discovery of Puget Sound*. Copyright © 1935 by Binford & Mort, Portland, Oregon.

Page 76 by John Muir, 1889. Source unknown.

Page 85 from *My Wilderness: The Pacific West* by William O. Douglas. Copyright © 1960 by Doubleday, New York.

Page 88 by Patrick Douglas. Published in *Saturday Review*, August 21, 1976.

Page 95 from "The Nature of Things" by Donald Culross Peattie. Published in *Audubon* magazine, 1941.

Page 100 from *Harper's Weekly*, June 20, 1891.

Page 104 from *Far Corner: A Personal View of the Pacific Northwest* by Stewart H. Holbrook. Copyright © 1952 by Macmillan, New York.

Page 115 from *Of Men and Mountains* by William O. Douglas. Copyright © 1950 by Harper & Brothers, New York.

Page 127 from *Evergreen Land: A Portrait of the State of Washington* by Nard Jones. Copyright © 1947 by Dodd, Mead & Co., New York.

Page 128 from *The Sea in the Forest* by Archie Binns. Copyright © 1953 by Doubleday, New York.

All other quotations are from the foreword by Paul Dorpat. Copyright © 1994 by Paul Dorpat.

Gulls rest on a surf-washed beach after a Pacific storm, Olympic National Park. RAY ATKESON.

"*It is seldom that you can find half a dozen of us together at one time to whom Washington means quite the same thing. It is a big state, and each of its parts is a bit different from the rest. Therefore, too, the sum of its parts means nothing, except that those parts are bound on the north by Canada, on the east by an imaginary line, on the south by the great Columbia, and on the west only by the vision of our people.*"

NARD JONES
Evergreen Land
A Portrait of the State of Washington, 1947

Mountain fireweed with Mount Rainier in the distance.   DARRELL GULIN.

"*Any one of the new peaks [in Washington's Cascade Mountains] would have been eternal landmarks. The grandest of them all was Mount Rainier, a perfect cone better than three miles high thundering out of the deepest note of the mountain calliope.*"

ARCHIE BINNS
The Sea in the Forest, 1953